Hope and Joy Will Find You

A GUIDED JOURNAL

BY

JAN MEYERS AND KAREN LEE-THORP

The Navigators is an international Christian organization. Our mission is to reach, disciple, and equip people to know Christ and to make Him known through successive generations. We envision multitudes of diverse people in the United States and every other nation who have a passionate love for Christ, live a lifestyle of sharing Christ's love, and multiply spiritual laborers among those without Christ.

NavPress is the publishing ministry of The Navigators. NavPress publications help believers learn biblical truth and apply what they learn to their lives and ministries. Our mission is to stimulate spiritual formation among our readers.

© 2003 by Jan Meyers

ISBN 1-57683-353-4

Cover design by Dan Jamison.
Cover and interior illustrations by Kari Alberg.
Creative Team: Nanci McAlister, Darla Hightower, Glynese Northam, Dan Jamison

The Weight of Glory by C.S. Lewis, copyright © C.S. Lewis Pte. Ltd. 1949. Extract reprinted by permission.

Unless otherwise identified, all Scripture quotations in this publication are taken from the *Holy Bible, New Living Translation*, (NLT) copyright © 1996. Used by permission of Tyndale House Publishers, Inc., Wheaton, Illinois 60189. All rights reserved. Other versions used include: the HOLY BIBLE: NEW INTERNATIONAL VERSION® (NIV®), Copyright © 1973, 1978, 1984 by International Bible Society, used by permission of Zondervan Publishing House, all rights reserved.

Printed in the United States of America

1 2 3 4 5 6 7 8 9 10 / 06 05 04 03

Contents

A LETTER OF *Introduction*

I don't know about you, but when I hear the word *hope*, I tend to think of the glorious endings of my favorite movies (Andy and Red's reunion, outside of prison, on the beach in Mexico in *The Shawshank Redemption* or the redemptive rescue in *Les Misérables*). Or the happily ever after of the grandest fairy tales. That's probably a good thing, because so much of hope has to do with something ending well. But as a woman who has placed her hope in the cross of Christ, I admit that there is a side to hope that I don't often acknowledge, let alone respond to: the side of hope that aches, groans, waits, perseveres, and languishes while it waits for the ending.

And when I hear the word *joy*, I tend to think of the exuberance I feel at the end of those movies and fairy tales. The happy ending speaks to something deep within my heart, and I say, "Yes!" and am filled with joy.

But the story of God is one where His children experience that joy *along the way*—during their soul's journey, *on the way* to the end of the story. So how do we discover that secret, knowing a true joy as we groan and wait and languish?

There is a little phrase in the eighth chapter of Romans that sums up the challenge of hope: "If you already have something, you don't have to hope for it." Think about it. Hope is all about longing for, waiting for, doing without but envisioning the day you'll have *the thing you want*.

Ah, that's the dilemma. Most of us, as Christian women, *don't know* what we want. I kid you not, it is an absolutely terrifying proposition for many of us to be asked to think about what we want because we've been taught that we should just be happy, and we spend lots of energy structuring our worlds, our lives, and our relationships in a way to convince ourselves that we are just fine, content. Then we put a Christian label on it and call it godly.

It's not. True biblical hope looks far more like the woman in Luke 7 who was willing to be a desperate, matted mess in her pursuit of what she wanted (what she had come to realize was the only thing that could quench her thirst, the only person who could love her fully) than our contemporary version of a hopeful woman. I say in *The Allure of Hope*, "We are far more disciplined than we are at rest, far more committed than winsome, far more 'nice' than passionate, far more dutiful than free. Far more weary than filled with hope." I see it everywhere—women who are "trying" to be hopeful, but who are really just worn out. If we "try" to be hopeful we will fail. If we "attempt" to be beautiful, we will feel inauthentic and deceptive. And if we do these things, there's no way we'll have true joy. We'll be obliged to put on a smiling mask that is a tragic sham.

The true route to joy is so different. In Isaiah 57 we are warned that in our wandering from the One who loves us, we will muster up all kinds of energy, never tiring of pursuing the things we think will keep us safe and satisfy us. God calls those things our idols. But then He says He wishes we would just faint, collapse, with Him.

Hopeful women are women who have fainted. They have said, "I cannot muster up any more false hope, and I cannot change myself into a godly Christian woman. I will faint and cry out to the God who both created me and cares about my heart. I will remember that He alone is the One who can sustain me as I ache over unfulfilled longings, as I groan with all creation, waiting for Him to rescue this weary world, as I persevere and allow my heart to be poured out for others, even as I am unfulfilled.

Perhaps, in ways we don't often consider, this is our soul's journey into true joy. Perhaps true joy comes as a surprising, mysterious companion (the fruit of the Spirit) as we hand over control of our lives to Jesus Christ.

This guided journal is a gift to you. With it, please hear an invitation to faint. To quit trying so hard. To surrender, not just to your failures or your need, but to the deep desires of your heart that you so often push away as frivolous. You know what I'm talking about—the little whispers when you think of the intimacy you long for, the connection you wish you had, the desire you have to be special and delighted in, without strings attached. It is my prayer that as you surrender to this (a surrender to admitting you were made by and for God), you'll find the joy of freedom that has been lurking underneath the piles of responsibility, disappointment, and pressure of your life. Wait for it; it will come. Hope and Joy will find you. And when He does, I pray you'll have the courage to simply let Him love you.

With Delight in Our Shared Hope, on Our Way to Joy,

Jan Meyers

HOW TO USE *This Journal*

Hope and Joy Will Find You is not a quest to find God but an opportunity to be found by God. At last you can quit trying so hard and let a lover pursue you.

The journey is divided into three stages. Each one uses a restaurant as a picture to help you explore hope: hope lost, hope counterfeited, and hope restored. In "Wanting but Not Having," you'll peer into the Restaurant of Hope — the place of feasting and joy for which your heart longs. You'll also feel what it's like to live in this fallen world, cast out the back door of the restaurant into a cold, dark alleyway. In "Avoiding the Ache," you'll examine the many ways you try to survive in the alleyway or force your way back into the restaurant. All this will prepare your heart for the third stage, in which you are "Found by God." As you become desperate enough to stop maneuvering, God will find you and feed you. With daily bread from God, you can live joyfully while you await the day when God will throw open the restaurant door.

The path you'll follow comes from *The Allure of Hope* by Jan Meyers. If you want to know more about any of the ideas you encounter in this journal, you may want to read *The Allure of Hope*.

This journal is designed to help you sit with your heart in God's presence. You can do that in whatever ways you find helpful. You can write in the journal, draw, cut out pictures from magazines and paste them in, use an exercise as springboard to prayer, or just read a section and think about it. You can journal on your own or talk about your thoughts with friends. Even if you don't consider yourself an artist, you might want to play with doodling or pasting pictures in your journal. Sometimes images say more to your heart than words. And don't worry if you don't have clear words for what you want to say. Nobody will be grading your essays. Sometimes a simple list or jumble of words will say it all.

Don't try to do the exercises perfectly. At the same time, do think deeply and respond honestly. To get the most out of this journal, you'll need to reflect on what's inside your heart. This can take some time and thought. If you find yourself freezing up, waiting for the "perfect" answer, then set aside your inner editor and just write. On the other hand, if you find yourself breezing through the exercises and learning nothing new, try slowing down and reflecting before you write.

Don't hurry yourself. Just make space to let your heart whisper or rage or weep or sing, and to let God find you there.

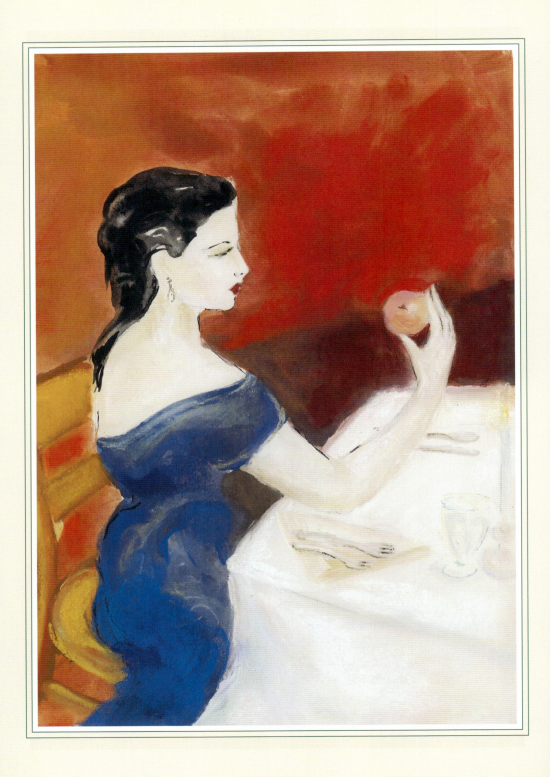

Wanting but Not Having

We begin our journey to joy by taking stock of our capacity for hope. Hope is eagerly looking forward to something glorious. Something glorious you desperately want but *don't have*. "For if you already have something, you don't need to hope for it. But if we look forward to something we don't have yet, we must wait patiently and confidently" (Romans 8:24-25).

If you have everything your heart desires, then you're in paradise. Our world, however, is not paradise. Therefore, if today your heart desires nothing it doesn't have, then you're not content; you're numb or dead. The apostle Paul said the normal state of a Spirit-filled Christian is to "groan to be released from pain and suffering. We, too, wait anxiously for that day when God will give us our full rights as his children, including the new bodies he has promised us" (Romans 8:23).

Too many Christian women have the impression that contentment means not groaning anymore. Paul declared, "I have learned the secret of being content in any and every situation" (Philippians 4:12, NIV), yet he boldly proclaimed his groaning. Think of it: contentment with what is while groaning for what can be and someday will be. Hope that blazes with desire, patience, and confidence. Does that describe you?

Possibly not. Perhaps you are far more disciplined than at rest, far more committed than winsome, far more "nice" than passionate, far more dutiful than free. Far more weary than filled with hope, desire, and eagerness.

You can't just try to hope. If you lack hope, and the eager desire and groaning that go with it, it's because thieves are sneaking into your heart and stealing your hope. To keep hope alive within you, you'll need to catch those thieves. Who are they?

THIEVES

Pay attention to what happens inside you when you read this story:

"The carpet feels warm underneath the dining room table as she lazily rolls over. Her six-year-old eyes take in the dust specks floating through the sun streaming from the window to her refuge. She is completely at rest, her mind freely wandering from a conversation with a neighborhood kitten to dreams of her birthday party. Her heart is a vast open place of dreaming, of knights and princes, horses and castles, lakes and sunshine, laughter and love. Her senses remember favorite meadows, bareback horse rides, velvet dresses, willow-tree branches. She hums a tune as she envisions her hero—she can see herself completely abandoned to the pursuit of the knight who comes to release her from her castle. She is beautiful, and she waits for him. She is well occupied as she waits. He will come. She waits for her daddy to be done with his work so she can run into his strong arms. She knows what it is she waits for. She is happy and content to do so; she knows she is not forgotten" (*The Allure of Hope,* p. 15).

While reading this, I

❑ Loved picturing the girl

❑ Wanted to hurry through it

❑ Rolled my eyes

❑ Wished I could be like that

❑ Felt sad

❑ Something else:

Reading about the little girl made me feel

Thieves

because

 sad
   cynical
    numb
  hungry
   inspired
   silly

If I imagine myself as that little girl, with the warmth of the sun and the freedom to daydream, what goes through my mind is

Thieves

Staying with this picture of yourself is often difficult. Give yourself some grace here. Jot down the sentences or thoughts or images that quickly interfere with your freedom to dream:

- ❑ Are they practical sentences? ("I really should be cleaning the office.")

- ❑ Are they condemning sentences? ("You are so ridiculous to be entertaining these childish thoughts. Grow up.")

- ❑ Are they pressured? ("I have to do this right. I have to get in touch with my dreams. I have to . . .")

- ❑ Are they despairing? ("What's the point?")

When I start to dream, my head goes to

Thieves

When I ask myself what I *really really* want, I

Writing in this journal feels

Thieves

I didn't know it would be so hard to dream. Why is that?

One thief who steals my dreams is named

Thieves

I don't know my thief's name, but some of the things he says to me when I start to daydream are

"Hope" is the thing with feathers—
That perches in the soul—
And sings the tunes without the words—
And never stops—at all—
—Emily Dickinson

I have *chosen* to allow this thief access to my heart. Why would I let someone rob me of hope and joy?

What would happen if I said no to this thief?

Thieves

DISAPPOINTMENT

"Why do we hesitate to live as openly and hopefully as a small child? Forgive such an obvious question. It is because we suffer. Each one of us can recall the moment when the childlike, open posture gave way to fear, disbelief, or disillusionment. Or perhaps we understand that living with childlike faith brings the subtle ache that does not go away. The groaning comes from unlimited vision of what could be" (*The Allure of Hope*, p. 18).

When did the thief first break into my heart?

When I was a little girl

I wanted something when I was little. Here's what happened.

Disappointment

I didn't like that, so I

Hope deferred makes the
heart sick,
but a longing fulfilled is a
tree of life.
—*Proverbs 13:12,* NIV

As a teen I was disappointed when

Disappointment

I dealt with that by

What happened to my heart was

19

When I remember these things, I

If you think in pictures, draw a picture of yourself looking disappointed. What would it look like to show God in the picture? Maybe wings wrapped around you?

Disappointment

BIRTH PAINS

Hope is about waiting. It's more like waiting for a baby to be born than like waiting to claim baggage after a flight. There's the thrill of anticipation but also an ache that grows if we pay attention to it. When you're pregnant, you often have to live through morning sickness, backaches, leg cramps, and long nights of wondering whether the baby will be healthy. As your due date nears, you're willing to do anything—even the agonizing hours of labor—to get to the goal of holding your newborn. The birthing room is messy, bloody, and hot, but it's all worth it when the baby comes.

Hope is like that—eager anticipation, but a long and often painful wait as well.

I'm waiting for

All creation has been groaning as in the pains of childbirth. . . . And even we Christians, although we have the Holy Spirit within us as a foretaste of future glory, also groan to be released from pain and suffering.
—Romans 8:22-23

When I wait, I usually

Birth Pains

When things are messy and painful, I often

If things aren't serene and orderly in my life, I

Birth Pains

These days, when I'm waiting for something, I

In our society, we have come to believe that discomfort means something is wrong. . . . [W]e are convinced that a rightly lived life must give us serenity, completion and fulfillment. Comfort means "right" and distress means "wrong."
—*Gerald May*

I'm waiting for something. I deal with it by

I faint with longing for your salvation;
but I have put my hope in your word.
—Psalm 119:81

Am I fainting with longing? Have I put my hope in God's Word?

Birth Pains

THE RESTAURANT OF HOPE

"Envision an exquisite five-star restaurant. You walk through the door and are gently jolted with the lull of conversation, the warmth of candlelight and luminous nooks, the mingled smells of several fine dishes. The room is festive and relaxing. The maitre d' ushers you to your table, causing you to feel welcomed, expected, desired. You feel the tension drain away as you prepare to enjoy friends and the anticipated meal.

"Looking up from your menu for a moment, you glance toward the kitchen and catch the eye of the chef, a kind-looking man. He acknowledges your gaze with a warm smile and a look that, in your restful state, says to you, 'I am preparing something wonderful just for you.' You feel a twinge of embarrassment, but it is quickly engulfed in the sheer delight of thinking that something is being prepared with you in mind.

"You love this place. Life feels right for a moment. How could he have known what you love? You wait and converse and laugh and drink and wait. And then it arrives—the spectacular dish. All are served, and with gratitude you savor your first bite. Heaven. Perfection. How did he do this?

"Suddenly, a tap on your shoulder. You turn to see the maitre d' standing behind you, grimfaced. 'I'm sorry, but I have to ask you to leave.' You are certain there is an emergency and you request the details, but none are given. 'No, I simply must ask you to leave. Please come with me.' His voice is commanding and direct. You are stunned and embarrassed but feel compelled to follow, at least to see what this interruption is about. The maitre d' ushers you past tables of glowing faces and candles, then through the kitchen, where you look for the chef but see only busboys. You are taken out the back door into the frigid night air, down the cement steps and into the alley behind the restaurant. Furious and confused, you demand an explanation, but all that is given in reply is the turn of the deadbolt lock.

"Silence.

"You are stunned. You are alone. Trashcans, oily puddles, and the steam from the sewer vent make up your new surroundings. Welcome to the alleyway" (*The Allure of Hope*, pp. 28-29).

Life has thrown me out into the alleyway. It happened like this.

The restaurant meal that was snatched from me was

Getting thrown into the alleyway felt

Now I feel

The Restaurant of Hope

"The most natural thing to do when life has jolted you into the alleyway is to think, *This is where my hope is lost. My sweet dream has been snatched away, and hope has been snatched away with it.* The wild reality of God, though, is that this is where hope begins. Hope begins when the memory of *what was* becomes a longing for *what is to be restored*" (*The Allure of Hope*, p. 29).

What I really miss is

The great thing about it was

The Restaurant of Hope

My best memories are

The Restaurant of Hope

When I remember, I feel

It's hard for me to stay with those memories because

What goes through my mind when I start to remember is

The Restaurant of Hope

Instead of remembering, I'd rather

       § eat
         § watch TV
           § exercise
      § stay busy
        § shop
          § go to a church meeting

THE PRETTY GOOD LIFE

From what you've read so far, you may get the impression that being thrown into the alleyway involves a major trauma—childhood abuse, a death, a major illness. *My life hasn't been that bad*, you may think. *No big tragedy. I guess I haven't experienced the alleyway.*

Not so. If your life doesn't seem like the alleyway, you haven't glimpsed the restaurant. The restaurant is Eden and heaven. In the restaurant for which you were made, God (the chef) would be intimately present with you; you would know the look in His eyes as He smiled at you. You would have a husband who deeply enjoyed and treasured you, or if you were single, your singleness would be a joy. Sex would be fantastic. Your children would be healthy, wise, and kind. You would have intimate friends who listened, added to your wisdom, and shared your labors. Your daily work would be a pleasure, a full expression of your creative gifts. You would never be bored by life's routines. There wouldn't even be others' suffering to cause you grief. You would be stunningly beautiful, inside and out.

If you think that's too much to want, turn to the section, "The Feast of Heaven." The Bible promises you a feast, a passionate love, glorious beauty, the end of every sorrow, and the fullness of joy. You were born not only to want this but to have it. If your wants are few, that's because you've learned to forget the restaurant of Eden, and you haven't learned to hope for the restaurant of heaven.

Until heaven, you live in a fallen world. Hungry and sorrowing people are everywhere. Even the best relationships aren't what they could be. You're getting older. Your parents and friends will die. So will you. It's natural to resist letting the pain of this life pierce you, but without being pierced by the pain, you can never know true hope or joy.

When I think about a world full of hungry and sorrowful people, I

The Pretty Good Life

I see the fallenness of the world in

I deal with life in a fallen world by

AN EXERCISE IN HOPE

If you really want to know how your heart responds to hope, go to a wonderful restaurant. Take your husband or a few friends. Let yourself go—no holds barred. If you're not used to spending that much money on yourself, make it your birthday present. Consider it psychotherapy or a spiritual retreat. Forget dieting, and abandon yourself to the experience.

From the moment you arrive at the restaurant, notice what's happening around you and inside you. Can you allow yourself to scan the menu with anticipation rather than guilt? Smell the smells. Drink in the atmosphere. When you take your first bite, let yourself think, "I really am hungry. I really do want this bite of food." Taste each bite. Savor your conversation over the meal. Enjoy your companions. What are you feeling?

Then, what is it like to leave at the end of the meal? What do you feel as you walk out? As you arrive home?

After you do this exercise, record your experience here.

When I contemplated going to the restaurant, I felt

When I walked into the restaurant, I noticed

During the meal

An Exercise in Hope

When I left the restaurant

How was this experience like the ways I respond in other situations when hope (wanting something good) stirs inside me?

An Exercise in Hope

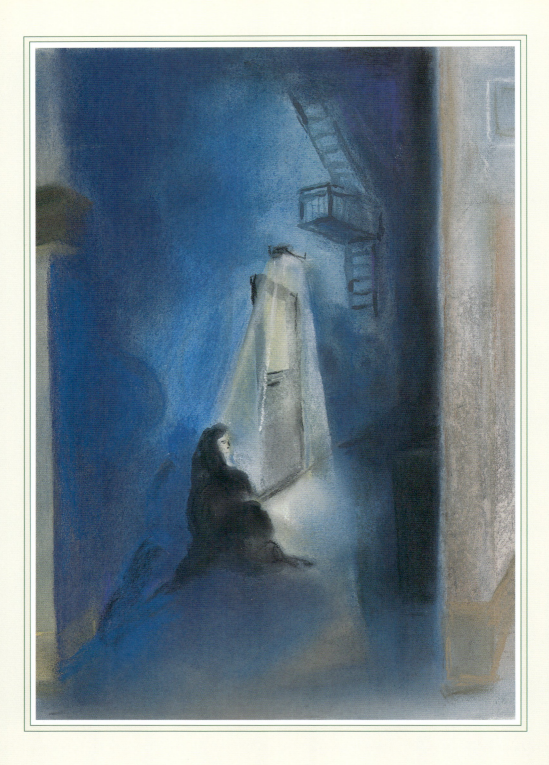

Avoiding the Ache

It doesn't feel good to want what we don't have unless we're *sure* it's only a matter of time until we get it and unless we have enough sustenance to manage until then. As long as our wedding day is set and we get to see our fiancé every day until then, we can survive a lengthy engagement (barely). But if he's in some other country with no phone and no fixed date of return, the wait is tough. For many of us out in the alleyway, we're not even sure we're engaged.

So how do we manage without what we long for? In this section, you'll explore the unique ways in which you deal with the alleyway. In the course of your life, you've learned an assortment of strategies for surviving. Some reflect resignation (Jan calls them "hovering"); others are more determined and driven (Jan calls those "clamoring"). Take some time to observe your chosen ways of hovering and clamoring. This section will help you identify and overcome them so you can choose a third option: hope. Hope is keeping your heart open and focused on the only sure future God has promised you. If your heart has long been closed or focused on the wrong goals, this section will get you ready to open it.

THE PATH OF HOVERING

When we're thrown out into the alleyway of life, we can respond in several ways. One option is to push aside memories of the restaurant, fling ourselves onto the nearest heating vent, and just try to survive the fierce cold. Hovering on the heating vent, wrapped in whatever coats and discarded blankets we can find, is a quick choice of fear, desperation, resignation, and self-contempt: *Of course. I could have predicted this. That fine meal was too good to be true. Forget about it. There's nothing to do now but figure out how to survive.*

For instance, when Jan's mother sank into depression, Jan abandoned her childhood whimsy for a hovering determination: "I would keep my mother alive. I would come up with some way to sustain her" (*The Allure of Hope*, p. 33).

When have I responded to disappointed hope with a determination to survive or to make someone else survive?

I resigned myself to

The Path of Hovering

I tried to survive by

The Path of Hovering

What happened was

Don't count on your warhorse
to give you victory—
for all its strength, it cannot
save you.
                    —Psalm 33:17

When Sandra left the job interview, she was full of hope for a wonderful position with the company. She was sure the supervisor liked her. When she heard nothing for two weeks, she phoned. The job had been given to someone else. No explanation. As she hung up the phone, she attacked herself: *How could I have been so stupid as to think I would be chosen? I should have known the supervisor was only humoring me! My answers to half his questions were lame. That first question. . . .* She felt humiliated for assuming the job would be hers.

I am such a fool. When am I going to learn not to get my hopes up?

I said this to myself when

The Path of Hovering

I said, *I knew it was too good to be true* when

I blamed myself for

To keep from having this happen again, I

The Path of Hovering

Blaming ourselves feels better than living with a disappointment that was out of our control. If we blame ourselves, at least it feels like there's something we can change to keep the worst from happening again.

I've tried to fix myself. Here's what I tried.

The Path of Hovering

What if the problem isn't me?

It's cold and scary out here in the alleyway! I have to do something! I have to take care of myself because there's nobody else I can trust.

I said this to myself when

The Path of Hovering

I thought there was nobody else I could trust because

44

Look, I refuse to be scared anymore. I'd rather be alone than deal with this kind of stuff. From now on, I take no trash from anyone. No one will ever take me for a ride again.

I felt this way when

The Path of Hovering

The results have been

45

I wish it weren't too good to be true. I wish I didn't feel I have to do this on my own. I wish there were someone who would fill me without smothering me, treasure me but not idolize me, receive my care without making me carry all the weight.

I wish

I wish

The Path of Hovering

I wish

When I think about these wishes, I feel

The Path of Hovering

"It is always easier to focus on what you can change than to face the questions welling up in your heart in the sorrow of what is beyond your control. . . . If we can find something about ourselves to get to work on, we are in control" (*The Allure of Hope,* pp. 35-36).

When desire is too painful, I numb it by

- ❑ eating
- ❑ dieting
- ❑ exercising
- ❑ getting my body pierced
- ❑ shopping
- ❑ doing ministry
- ❑ devouring romance novels
- ❑ gossiping
- ❑ touring porn websites
- ❑ losing myself in a relationship that's going nowhere
- ❑ watching TV
- ❑ having a Christian tea
- ❑ working
- ❑ driving my kids to appointments
- ❑ listening to music
- ❑
- ❑

The Path of Hovering

What is hovering like for you? Draw a picture of yourself literally hovering over a steam grate or doing whatever you do when you're in survival mode. Or make a collage by cutting out words and images from magazines that depict how you hover. What faces remind you of yourself? What tools help you survive? How do you block out the thoughts of the restaurant you really want?

The Path of Hovering

FACING THE FALL

We live in the alleyway of a fallen world. But hovering leads us to pretend we don't. Many of us confuse faith in Christ with maneuvering to avoid the consequences of Eve's sin in Eden. Her sin saddled us with pain in childbirth and an aching desire to make our husbands love us and do what we want (Genesis 3:16). We suffer pain when we give life, and we feel compelled to control others so they won't let us down. We long to be lovers and lifegivers, but the pain leads us astray. We need to face this gap between who we long to be and who we are.

Am I

❑ rigid

❑ too controlled

❑ trying to convince myself that I'm content

❑ pushing myself to believe God is good

❑ trying to control my surroundings and my relationships

❑ compulsive about living within the lines in my relationships

❑ silent, with little to offer

❑ saccharin, syrupy, too sweet

❑ determined to be known as a godly woman

Am I

❑ human

❑ relaxed

❑ honest with God about what I think of Him

❑ genuine

❑ convinced that I can't take care of myself

❑ full of longings

❑ driven to God by loneliness

How does the man in my life let me down?

What do I do to try to keep him from letting me down?

*Then [God] said to the
woman, "You will bear
children with intense pain
and suffering. And though
your desire will be for your
husband, he will be your master."*
—Genesis 3:16

What kind of woman would I like to be with my husband sexually?

I'd like to be that woman, but I shut down when

Facing the Fall

What kind of woman would I like to be with my friends?

Faeing the Fall

I'd like to be that woman, but I shut down when

Who would I like to be in my work and calling?

I fall short of being that woman when

Facing the Fall

Oh, what a miserable person I am! Who will free me from this life that is dominated by sin? Thank God! The answer is in Jesus Christ our Lord.
—Romans 7:24-25

Dear God, please

Facing the Fall

What kind of mother would I like to be?

Facing the Fall

I find myself not being that woman when

How would I like to express my creativity?

Facing the Fall

I don't do it because

Cowards die many times before their deaths;
The valiant never taste of death but once.
—William Shakespeare

"A gentle and quiet spirit has a natural, earthy beauty. It's human. It has the power to win others to belief in God's goodness (1 Peter 3:4-6). It comes from a vulnerable posture that surrenders all fear of how a man or anyone else will handle us" (*The Allure of Hope*, p. 45).

What would I be like if I surrendered my fear of how people will handle me?

Facing the Fall

In all these ways, as wife and lover, as friend, as mother, in work and creativity, I'm not the woman I'd like to be. There's no point in pretending. I can't try harder. Jesus, I'm desperate. Let me rest in Your strength. Let me be desperate in Your presence. I want to give life, to open my heart to others, to offer wisdom. But I'm so thirsty. Find me in spite of my wandering heart. Speak to our Father on my behalf. Tell Him. . . .

Facing the Fall

If we confess our sins to him,
he is faithful and just to
forgive us and to cleanse us
from every wrong.
— 1 John 1:9

INSTEAD OF HOVERING

Here are some pictures of what it's like to choose to hope and ache rather than hover. What happens inside you when you think about each one?

You're strolling on a magnificent seacoast. You watch the surf pound onto the rocks and the breeze sweep through fields of lilac and yellow flowers. You breathe in the aroma of Eden and carry the memory with you into your next encounter with your aging mother.

You experience an abandoned and connected time of lovemaking with your husband. You enter into it without resignation, fear, or warning to protect your heart, even though you know he'll spend Sunday afternoon lost in TV football.

You laugh uproariously with dear friends. It's a loud, strong laugh from deep inside you.

Instead of Hovering

Your husband dies, leaving you alone with children to care for. You don't pretend you trust God in this horrible situation. Instead, you pour out your fear, doubt, and questions to Him. Instead of pursuing Him, you allow Him to pursue you. You keep choosing to open your heart to God, your children, and the people around you, even though opening your heart hurts terribly.

You confront your heart's determination to avoid loneliness and desire. You acknowledge the many and varied ways you try to control people and situations. You allow God to capture your heart in the midst of your hardheartedness.

Instead of Hovering

Instead of hovering today, I want to

For many of us, learning about hovering is just one more reason to feel pressure. We think, "I guess I need to work harder to stop hovering." We sigh. "I guess I need to put some effort into being relaxed, honest with God, genuine, and full of hopeful longings. I should have known I wasn't doing the Christian life well enough. Somehow I have to figure out how to be hopeful without becoming discontent or some other thing I shouldn't be."

But that's the same old story, isn't it? We're already hunkering down to figure out how to survive this new twist on the alleyway experience. Our hopes of being good Christian women have been dashed, and we're telling ourselves we should never have wasted our time hoping we were good enough. Our response to hovering is more hovering! Alas, who can free us from this bondage?

When I realized what a hovering mess I am, I felt

Instead of Hovering

I decided to

What if God loves me even while I'm doing all this ridiculous hovering? What if He doesn't need me to stop all that in order for Him to be delighted with me?

Instead of Hovering

Instead of trying hard to stop hovering, I will

O Israel, hope in the LORD;
for with the LORD there is unfailing love
and an overflowing supply of salvation.
—Psalm 130:7

Spend a day watching how you respond to situations. If you catch yourself hovering (sighing with resignation at some frustration, telling yourself you're a fool for hoping, frantically trying to pull things together, gritting your teeth to survive, talking with irony or cynicism, or being bland instead of warm and openhearted), resist the urge to condemn yourself. This is a day to notice, not a day to try harder.

Jesus, I hovered today. Here's what I did.

Instead of Hovering

I tried so hard to be different, but I was my usual self. I felt

Jesus, when You see me hovering, what does Your face look like? Do You frown with frustration? Roll Your eyes? Smile gently and tenderly? Do You love me anyway?

Instead of Hovering

The LORD still waits for you to come to him so he can show you his love and compassion. For the LORD is a faithful God. Blessed are those who wait for him to help them.
—Isaiah 30:18

If you can't describe Jesus' face, try drawing it. Or cut a picture out of a maga-
zine that has a face that reminds you of Jesus.

Instead of Hovering

THE PATH OF CLAMORING

When we're thrown out into the alleyway of life, we sometimes hover on a steam grate, trying to survive. It's too painful even to remember the restaurant, never mind trying to get back in. When we hover, we blame ourselves for our predicament.

At other times we react differently. We march up the steps to the kitchen door, pound on it, and demand to be let back into the restaurant. We're furious. We blame the restaurant owner. When the door doesn't open, we set about devising strategies to force or manipulate our way back in. This is the path of clamoring.

Oh no they don't! . . . I belong in that restaurant! . . . At least I thought I did. . . . I have to be there or I'll die. . . . Besides, I deserve to be there, don't I? . . . I will run up those steps and pound on the door until I'm let back in. . . .

"I have to be there or I'll die." When have I said that?

I deserve to be in there, don't I?

The Path of Clamoring

Maybe I'm not beautiful enough to have what I long for. I doubt my beauty because

Maybe I don't have enough inside me to offer, so I'm not good enough for those people. I'm afraid this might be true because

What can I do to change myself so they'll let me in?

The Path of Clamoring

Ways I've tried to change myself:

To make a man love me, I've

To make people like me, I've

The Path of Clamoring

To make people admire me, I've

To make myself beautiful enough on the outside, I've

To make myself beautiful enough on the inside, I've

72

What does each of these people want me to be?

husband/boyfriend

parents

boss

The Path of Clamoring

church leaders

friend

Do I give in and try to be what they want?

Claire was an artist, philosopher, and poet by nature. But she learned early in life that impassioned questions and artistic expression didn't change her world or get her the restaurant meal she longed for. So she entered the religious world and got very, very good at it. She figured out what people wanted. Claire married a successful businessman who was an elder in a prominent church. She became the right-hand woman to a popular Bible teacher. Claire began to teach also. She was disciplined in Scripture memory and study, always (rightfully) concerned to handle the Word carefully. She made people's heads spin with her knowledge, and she asked of others the same level of mastery.

How are you like or unlike Claire?

The Path of Clamoring

I'm determined and driven. My body and my heart are always moving, doing whatever it takes to get . . .

The Path of Clamoring

The result is

I'm driving. In the van next to my car, I see a mother and three children. She seems so perky and energetic. I think

The Path of Clamoring

I'm in a small group. Another woman shares what's happening in her life. I'm frustrated that I'm not like her. I tell myself

I'm having a heated discussion with my husband/boyfriend. He backs away. I push harder because I want

I look at a stunningly beautiful woman, and I think

The Path of Clamoring

And on that cheek, and o'er that brow,
So soft, so calm, yet eloquent
The smiles that win, the tints that glow,
But tell of days in goodness spent,
A mind at peace with all below,
A heart whose love is innocent
    —Lord Byron

When I read Byron's poem, I

I don't want to be one of the masses. I want to be one of the special ones. If only I were:

- ❑ richer
- ❑ more beautiful
- ❑ famous
- ❑ higher up in my career
- ❑ the mother of
- ❑ the wife of
- ❑ the center of attention in
- ❑ a leader in
- ❑
- ❑
- ❑

The Path of Clamoring

If only my husband would do what I want in

If only

When someone else is in the spotlight, I feel

The Path of Clamoring

It's hard for me to "Rejoice with those who rejoice" (Romans 12:15) because

Envy, slothful vice,
Never makes its way in lofty characters,
But, like the skulking viper, creeps and crawls
Close to the ground.
—Ovid

THIS IS ME CLAMORING:

(Sketch yourself, paste in a photo of yourself, or cut out a series of pictures from magazines that represent the Clamoring You.)

The Path of Clamoring

INSTEAD OF CLAMORING

Clamoring compels us to possess or remake our beauty. The alternative is to allow our true, mysterious, unmanageable beauty—the beauty of a redeemed heart—to be revealed. This is what the apostle Paul means when he speaks of unveiled faces in 2 Corinthians 3:18. Unveiled faces are exposed, vulnerable, and desperate. They reflect God's heart for beauty to be restored and displayed at all costs. An unveiled woman might:

❑ Weep for the way she has underestimated her husband

❑ Be unable to contain her joy over her child's inquisitive questioning of the world

❑ Know her tendency to rage and stop for a moment to plead with God to love through her

What would my unveiled face look like at work?

And we, who with unveiled faces
reflect the Lord's glory, are being
transformed into his likeness with
ever-increasing glory, which comes
from the Lord, who is the Spirit.
—2 Corinthians 3:18, NIV

With my husband?

With my family?

With my friends?

At church?

Why don't I unveil in front of people? What am I afraid might happen?

Instead of Clamoring

To be nobody-but-yourself,
in a world that is doing its
best night and day to make
you everybody else, means to
fight the hardest battle any
human being can fight and
never stop fighting.
—e.e. cummings

We try to re-create ourselves because we think we're not beautiful enough, strong enough, accomplished enough to be wanted as we are. We think we were thrown out of the restaurant because of some deficiency that we have to fix. We fail to look outside ourselves for the answer because we're sure it must come from something we can do or become.

We don't realize we're already wanted. God says to us what He said to Jerusalem, His betrothed:

> *O storm-battered city, troubled and desolate! I will rebuild you on a foundation of sapphires and make the walls of your houses from precious jewels. I will make your towers of sparkling rubies and your gates and walls of shining gems. I will teach all your citizens, and their prosperity will be great. You will live under a government that is just and fair. Your enemies will stay far away; you will live in peace. Terror will not come near. If any nation comes to fight you, it will not be because I sent them to punish you. Your enemies will always be defeated because I am on your side. (Isaiah 54:11-15)*

If God is saying this to me, I

Instead of Clamoring

Does God really feel this way about me even while I'm doing all this ugly clamoring? Don't I have to pull myself together right now and quit clamoring?

Instead of trying hard to stop clamoring today, I will

LORD, sustain me as you promised, that I may live!
Do not let my hope be crushed.
—Psalm 119:116

It's hard for me to imagine I'm not under pressure to fix all this. Don't I need to get busy repenting?

Instead of Clamoring

If repentance isn't trying hard to stop doing all this bad stuff, then what could it possibly be?

There are things I can't fix. I can only weep over them with a broken heart for what I've done. My only hope is mercy. Does God forgive me?

Instead of Clamoring

Have mercy on me, O God,
because of your unfailing love.
Because of your great compassion,
blot out the stain of my sins.
—Psalm 51:1

Found by God

What moves us to pause our hovering and clamoring, and hope desperately for someone to rescue us in the alleyway? Failure, perhaps. Perhaps we see that our many maneuverings have not filled our hungry stomachs. But the only sure cure for hovering and clamoring is the discovery that the restaurant chef sees us and longs for us even when we behave foolishly. One day he will open the door and welcome us back into the restaurant. In the meantime, it is not out of spite or unconcern that he leaves us in the alleyway. In fact, his own son has endured the alleyway on our behalf.

Hope is not a search to find God in the alleyway. Hope is stopping our maneuverings long enough to be found by God.

HOPING TO BE FOUND

Hope is remembering the meal in the restaurant, aching to have it back, and yearning to be found in the alleyway. Hope is:

❑ A child remembering last Christmas and anticipating the next Christmas — in September.

❑ An eighty-seven-year-old woman remembering what it was like to climb mountains when she was young and praying quietly for God to let her come home.

❑ A single woman aching to be married yet investing heart and soul in the lives of both single and married friends.

❑ A wife tenderly inviting her husband to join her for a dinner alone together, knowing he has been preoccupied with work for some time.

When did I hope as a child?

What did I hope for in my marriage when I was a new bride?

Hoping to be Found

What have I hoped for in my marriage this week?

I hoped when

I hoped when

Hoping to be Found

I hoped when

The hard thing about hoping like this is

If I suppress hope in these situations, then

When I had lost all hope, I
turned my thoughts once
more to the LORD. *And my*
earnest prayer went out to
you in your holy Temple.
—Jonah 2:7

ADMITTING I'M LOST

Many of us want to jump to the doctrine that God has found us. We're saved!
But standing in the alleyway, clenching our teeth, closing our eyes, and pro-
claiming a silent mantra—"I am loved, I am loved, I am not forgotten"—is not
the route to a vision of God. Instead of singing worship songs we don't believe,
we need to tell God what we really think of the way He's handling our lives.
God invites us to express the stark emotions of the Psalms:

> O LORD, God of my salvation,
> I have cried out to you day and night.
> Now hear my prayer;
> listen to my cry.
> For my life is full of troubles, . . .
> I am forgotten,
> cut off from your care.
> You have thrust me down to the lowest pit,
> into the darkest depths. . . .
> You have caused my friends to loathe me;
> you have sent them all away.
> I am in a trap with no way of escape.
> My eyes are blinded by my tears.
> Each day I beg for your help, O LORD;
> I lift my pleading hands to you for mercy. . . .
> O LORD, I cry out to you.
> I will keep on pleading day by day.
> O LORD, why do you reject me?
> Why do you turn your face away from me?
> I have been sickly and close to death since my youth.
> I stand helpless and desperate before your terrors. . . .
> You have taken away my companions and loved ones;
> only darkness remains.
> —Psalm 88

When we admit the confusion and rage in our hearts, then our humble God can find us and offer us tastes of His feast.

If I could say anything to God, it would be

Admitting I'm Lost

I would like to ask God

I'm lost. I wish God would find me. O God, please

Admitting I'm Lost

Remember your promise to me,
for it is my only hope.
—Psalm 119:49

DAILY BREAD

The alleyway is the place where we lost hope and joy. It can also be the place where we regain hope and joy. We begin by softening our hearts enough to receive daily bread from God. We've tried to feed ourselves on garbage: TV, shopping, work, compulsive relationships, ministry, and a thousand other things. But if we pause, we can see that God is offering us nourishing food even here, in the alleyway.

Daily bread comes to us in:

❑ Sunsets

❑ The night sky

❑ The soil in our hands as we dig and plant

❑ Lingering over coffee with a friend

❑ Listening, really listening, to someone

❑ Strolling through an art gallery with our kids

❑ Relishing a quiet time of worship

❑ Taking the hand of an elderly person

How have I been fed today?

The sky is the daily bread
of the eyes.
—Ralph Waldo Emerson

"I woke up one morning with a piercing awareness that I didn't have any children begging me to make waffles, nor a lover in my bed. I was tempted, for a moment, to crawl back under the covers and make up a dream about a man I care a lot about who has been kind to me. Can you hear how doing so would have been a surrender to boredom and deceit?

Instead of boredom, manna [bread] came. I walked out into the dawn to find whispers of red clouds strewn along the horizon. Just above a row of cottonwood trees, a red fox was curled up in the snow, waiting for the first stream of sunlight—she also was waiting. I had a long, uncomfortable talk with God. I reminded Him of how lonely I am, and He held me for a while. Did this manna eradicate my desire? No, it deepened it. But it deepened it toward the heart of God instead of away from Him" (*The Allure of Hope,* pp. 86-87).

What goes through my mind when I read this story?

What makes me want to crawl back under the covers is

Daily Bread

I think God might come to me in that situation if I

I don't think I'm getting fed enough. I think it's because

Daily Bread

Presence is what we are all starving for. Real presence!
We are too busy to be present, too blind to see the nour-
ishment and salvation in the crumbs of life, the experi-
ences of each moment. Yet the secret of daily life is this:
There are no leftovers!
—Macrina Wiederkehr

How could I be more available for daily bread from God?

Daily Bread

Hope is definitely not the same thing as optimism. It is not the conviction that something will turn out well, but the certainty that something makes sense, regardless of how it turns out.
— Václav Havel

We are so aware that life is a battle. But we often think it's up to us to fight the forces of evil. In reality, the battle is between Christ and the Enemy, and the prize is our hearts. God calls to us: "Remember what I intended for you. Let Me fight your enemies (including your own treatment of your heart) that have robbed you of your joy. Rest in Me as you recall the promise that I will find you" (*The Allure of Hope*, p. 92).

God is fighting against evil to win my heart. What do I think about that?

Daily Bread

I've been trying to fight

Daily Bread

The battle has left me

What if I rested and let God fight?

What do I fear might happen if I let go of the distractions I'm so busy with and poured out my deepest heart to God?

Daily Bread

I long to:

❑ Matter to someone

❑ Have an adventure

❑ Be forgiven

❑ Do something brave and heroic

❑ Be looked at with eyes that are thrilled with me

❑

❑

❑

The church often unwittingly offers us counterfeit bread: programs, steps, out-lines, formulas, and advice. But church activity won't bring us the life we hope for if we focus on order, discipline, and involvement. It's false bread to set our hope on our prowess as great Christians, our commitment, or our stand on vari-ous political and moral issues. We need to be famished for Christ Himself.

Counterfeit bread exchanges the prophet's cry:

> *"Is anyone thirsty? Come and drink—even if you have no money! Come, take your choice of wine or milk—it's all free! Why spend your money on food that does not give you strength? Why pay for food that does you no good? Listen, and I will tell you where to get food that is good for the soul!" (Isaiah 55:1-2)*

for a pitiful whimper:

> *"Come on in and join us as we work really hard to come up with a consistent perspective on life. We're not really very thirsty; we're too busy to notice if we are, anyway. If you'd like to provide a meal for yourself while you work with us, that would be great—that's what most of us have done, brought a bag lunch." (The Allure of Hope, p. 154)*

What kind of food have I been getting at church?

Daily Bread

What would it look like to feast on Christ? Would commitment and moral issues go out the window?

Daily Bread

What I long for from church is

When I think about trusting God to provide bread for me tomorrow, I

Daily Bread

Those who sow in tears
will reap with songs of joy.
He who goes out weeping,
carrying seed to sow,
will return with songs of joy,
carrying sheaves with him.
—Psalm 126:5-6, NIV

THE FEAST OF HEAVEN

If daily bread were all we could ever look forward to, we would rightfully be discouraged. "If we have hope in Christ only for this life, we are the most miserable people in the world" (1 Corinthians 15:19). Daily bread sustains us, but it also makes us even hungrier for the feast of heaven.

God makes huge promises about what is to come. He wants us to imagine our future because a confident hope of the future enables us to risk and love in the present. We can endure the pain of today knowing that tomorrow will bring joy.

For many of us, though, heaven isn't much to look forward to. That's because we've been given such bland pictures of what it will be like. John Eldredge explains:

> But of course we aspire to happiness we can enjoy now. Our hearts have no place else to go. We have made a nothing of eternity. If I told you that your income would triple next year, and that European vacation you've wanted is just around the corner, you'd be excited, hopeful. The future would look promising. It seems possible, desirable. But our ideas of heaven, while possible, aren't all that desirable. Whatever it is we think is coming in the next season of our existence, we don't think it is worth getting all that excited about. We make nothing of eternity by enlarging the significance of this life and by diminishing the reality of what the next life is all about.
>
> Nearly every Christian I have spoken with has some idea that eternity is an unending church service. After all, the Bible says that the saints 'worship God in heaven,' and without giving it much more thought we have settled on an image of the never-ending sing-along in the sky, one great hymn after another, forever and ever, amen.
>
> And our heart sinks. Forever and ever? That's it? That's the good news? And then we sigh and feel guilty that we are not more "spiritual." We lose heart, and we turn once more to the present to find what life we can.
>
> (*The Journey of Desire,* pp. 110-111).

When I think of heaven as an unending church service, I feel

Do I even like worshiping God?

Thank God, heaven won't be an endless church service! The Bible gives us much more sensual, active pictures of life in the kingdom of heaven.

Following are a series of paintings of your future. What happens inside you as you read each one? Which ones speak most to your heart?

In Jerusalem, the LORD *Almighty will spread a wonderful feast for everyone around the world. It will be a delicious feast of good food, with clear, well-aged wine and choice beef. In that day he will remove the cloud of gloom, the shadow of death that hangs over the earth. He will swallow up death forever! The Sovereign* LORD *will wipe away all tears. He will remove forever all insults and mockery against his land and people. The* LORD *has spoken! (Isaiah 25:6-8)*

The Feast of Heaven

What foods would I like to have at the feast?

The Feast of Heaven

Who would I like to sit next to and talk to at the feast?

How will that feel?

I heard a loud shout from the throne, saying, "Look, the home of God is now among his people! He will live with them, and they will be his people. God himself will be with them. He will remove all of their sorrows, and there will be no more death or sorrow or crying or pain. For the old world and its evils are gone forever." And the one sitting on the throne said, "Look, I am making all things new!" And then he said to me, "Write this down, for what I tell you is trustworthy and true."
(Revelation 21:3-5)

What will it be like to live with God right there, face to face?

"You have stolen my heart, my sister, my bride;
you have stolen my heart
with one glance of your eyes,
with one jewel of your necklace."
(*Song of Songs 4:9,* NIV)

What will it be like to have Christ look at me and say that to me?

"Well done, my good and faithful servant. You have been faithful in handling this small amount, so now I will give you many more responsibilities. Let's celebrate together!"
(Matthew 25:21)

"[N]othing can eliminate from the parable the divine *accolade,* 'Well done, thou good and faithful servant.' . . . I suddenly remembered that no one can enter heaven except as a child; and nothing is so obvious in a child—not a conceited child, but in a good child—as its great and undisguised pleasure in being praised. . . . And that is enough to raise our thoughts to what may happen when the redeemed soul, beyond all hope and nearly beyond belief, learns at last that she has pleased Him whom she was created to please. There will be no room for vanity then. She will be free from the miserable illusion that it is her doing. . . . If God is satisfied with the work, then the work may be satisfied with itself. . . . To please God . . . to be a real ingredient in the divine happiness . . . to be loved by God, not merely pitied, but delighted in as an artist delights in his work or a father in a son—it seems impossible, a weight or burden of glory which our thoughts can hardly sustain. But so it is."

—*C.S. Lewis,* The Weight of Glory

What might it be like to find that even with all my mistakes I have pleased God?

When God says to me, "Well done!" His eyes will look

The Feast of Heaven

And I'll feel

And my past failures will

If I knew for sure today that God was pleased with me, then

The Feast of Heaven

What pleases God?

116

What causes me to doubt that God is delighted with me?

What reassures me?

The Feast of Heaven

What do Jesus' eyes look like? When I look into Jesus' eyes, I see

The Feast of Heaven

When the accusers heard this, they slipped away one by one, beginning with the oldest, until only Jesus was left in the middle of the crowd with the woman. Then Jesus stood up again and said to her, "Where are your accusers? Didn't even one of them condemn you?" "No, Lord," she said. And Jesus said, "Neither do I. Go and sin no more."
—John 8:9-11

Everyone who is victorious will eat of the manna that has been hidden away in heaven. And I will give to each one a white stone, and on the stone will be engraved a new name that no one knows except the one who receives it.
(*Revelation 2:17*)

Your new name is the identity Jesus is giving you. The true you, who only Jesus and you will fully know. Imagine what your identity might be.

What do I already know that Jesus says is true of me?

The Feast of Heaven

In my wildest dreams, I hope my name will include

For me, the best parts of heaven will be

The Feast of Heaven

When I think about heaven, I feel

Joy wants the eternity of all things, wants deep,
wants deep eternity.
—Friedrich Nietzsche

How do you envision heaven? Draw or paste in images that evoke your hopes for heaven.

The Feast of Heaven

Thinking about heaven can be uncomfortable. For one thing, the Bible's images, such as feasts and marriage, are so earthy. If we're not used to letting ourselves dream guiltlessly about fabulous food and sex, we can feel awkward when the Bible invites us to do just that. Our desires for food, sex, and everything else are meant to point beyond themselves to the ultimate intimacy and ecstasy with God and His people. We need more, stronger desire, not less.

The other discomfort is that at some point we must turn from our dreams of heaven to our present lives. The alleyway looks so much grayer when we remember the restaurant — that's why we put the restaurant out of our minds in the first place. How can we bear earth if we let ourselves long for heaven?

I want heaven now.

The Feast of Heaven

If I can't have heaven now, I'll

What am I going to do while I wait for heaven? Shall I just drift along and survive on dreams until I can be with God? If I do that, I'll gain

The Feast of Heaven

The costs of doing that will be

LIFE UNTIL HEAVEN

If heaven will be so good, why does God want us on earth now? For one thing, earth is a training camp where we become fit for heaven. For another, earth is where we give life to others. We bear children; we draw people to faith and hope through our words and actions.

❑ On earth we bear and raise children so they can choose God.

❑ We give life to others by showing by our words and actions that God is good.

❑ We support each other in becoming and being life-givers.

Compassion is central to our calling as life-givers. "Compassion is called out of us when we see situations where there is an obvious lack of something or someone life-giving. It calls us to ache, mostly because we are forced to long for the restoration of whatever or whoever is absent. For those of us who have tasted the riches of Christ, compassion calls us to want to extend His heart into the situation, to be ministers of reconciliation and restoration. Of course, we can choose to enter these situations with nothing more than a haughty, sacrificial stance in which we say to ourselves, *It sure is a good thing I am here helping out. And now that I think about it, I'm an amazing and wonderful person for giving up my time and energy to be here*" (*The Allure of Hope*, pp. 155-156).

The antidote to haughty sacrifice is allowing ourselves to mourn the absence of love for God in our own hearts. The lack of God we see "out there" is paralleled by the lack we know "in here." This stunning awareness moves us "to long for God's presence to intrude into the most common of situations—a conversation with a friend that is stuck at mere surface chatter, a relationship that has been settling for civility while avoiding deeper issues of the heart," a worship service where people sing about God rather than connecting with God (*The Allure of Hope*, p. 160).

A situation where I notice something life-giving is missing is

Life Until Heaven

What I ache to see in that situation or relationship is

If I wanted to play the hero or martyr, I would

Life Until Heaven

But when I see what's missing in my own heart, my attitude toward this situation becomes

Life Until Heaven

I think the best thing for me to do is

Sometimes I think I'm too much of a mess to offer anything in these situations. But God probably wants

Another aspect of living in hope is *tender perseverance*. In the harsh winds of the alleyway, many women harden. We can become church ladies who will argue over the color of the sanctuary carpet. Responding to hope, though, takes the edge off perseverance. We keep on keeping on, but with passion and softness. "It's the difference between the woman known for being a bulldog and the woman known for having chutzpah" (*The Allure of Hope,* p. 162).

What will it look like for me to persevere *tenderly*?

Life Until Heaven

"Persevere, but persevere *toward Me.* Let Me reveal your story to you, and then let Me show you how it fits into Mine. Let Me show you how much I trust your heart to finish this path, because you are Mine" (*The Allure of Hope,* p. 167).

Jesus, I

Life Until Heaven

*If you find someone who has
lived life fully and is still full of life,
you have found a treasure.
Learn from him or her.*
—Macrina Wiederkehr

We're not here in the alleyway just to wait for the restaurant door to open. We're here to learn how to love one another in the alleyway, so we'll be ready for an eternity of loving one another in the restaurant.

What is the greatest thing that has been transformed in me because of an alleyway experience?

Life Until Heaven

What have I learned in the alleyway that helps me love?

What opportunities do I have to use what I've learned in the alleyway to love others?

Life Until Heaven

Until we learn to sit at one another's feet, we will starve at our lavish banquet tables.
—Macrina Wiederkehr

Jesus, thank you for my life here on earth because

Life Until Heaven

"I hope God will tell His story through me. I hope my hard heart will soften. I hope His love shows through me in spite of myself. I hope my life will make a difference in this weary world, bringing refreshment and life to those without it. I hope to be surprised as God's glory shows up unexpectedly. I hope to have eyes to see His kindness and His humor. I hope to draw out the heart of a person with curiosity rather than alienate with my spiritual pride" (*The Allure of Hope,* pp. 118-119).

What I most hope for my life here and now is

Life Until Heaven

Without action, we are dreamers who will eventually stray into fantasy. To act for the sake of the future is to risk our present for a vague unknown. It is to stretch ourselves outside the parameters of safety that often serve as our fortress and prison.
—Dan Allender

Jesus introduced His own ministry by quoting these words from the prophet
Isaiah:

> The Spirit of the Sovereign LORD is on me,
>   because the LORD has anointed me
>   to preach good news to the poor.
> He has sent me to bind up the brokenhearted,
>   to proclaim freedom for the captives
>   and release from darkness for the prisoners,
> to proclaim the year of the LORD's favor
>   and the day of vengeance of our God,
> to comfort all who mourn,
>   and provide for those who grieve in Zion—
> to bestow on them a crown of beauty
>   instead of ashes,
> the oil of gladness
>   instead of mourning,
> and a garment of praise
>   instead of a spirit of despair.
> They will be called oaks of righteousness,
>   a planting of the LORD
>   for the display of his splendor.
> —Isaiah 61:1-3, NIV; compare Luke 4:18-19

This passage encourages me to believe that the Lord will

Life Until Heaven

JOY

When we've come this far, our thoughts are filled with compassion, with tender perseverance, with the wonders God has done in our hearts as we've given up trying so hard and begun to eat His daily bread. Our thoughts stray to that which awaits us when the restaurant door opens, even while we fix them on the presence of Jesus here and now. We hardly notice that, almost as a byproduct, joy has begun to well up from deep within us. We still groan with waiting, but the presence of Jesus, the opportunity to give life, and the anticipation of what's to come give our groaning this flavor called joy.

I think I've tasted joy when

Instead of their shame
my people will receive a double portion,
and instead of disgrace
they will rejoice in their inheritance;
and so they will inherit a double portion in their land,
and everlasting joy will be theirs.
—Isaiah 61:7, NIV

When anxiety was great within me,
your consolation brought joy to my soul.
Psalm 94:19, NIV

I've seen joy in other people. It looked like

What gives me joy is

Joy

May the God of hope fill you with all joy and peace as you trust in him, so that you may overflow with hope by the power of the Holy Spirit.
—*Romans 15:13,* NIV

Actually, I don't have much joy yet. I think right now I'm

Joy

What keeps me going is

*I tell you the truth, you will weep
and mourn while the world rejoices.
You will grieve, but your grief will
turn to joy. A woman giving birth to
a child has pain because her time has
come; but when her baby is born she
forgets the anguish because of her
joy that a child is born into the
world. So with you: Now is your
time of grief, but I will see you again
and you will rejoice, and no one will
take away your joy.*
　　　　　—John 16:20-22, NIV

The last time I experienced what I think was joy was when

Joy

When I picture joy in my life today

Bring joy to your servant,
for to you, O LORD,
I lift up my soul.
—*Psalm 86:4,* NIV

My prayer for joy:

Jesus, I trust You. I know one day you'll open the restaurant door for me. And I know you are with me right now, providing daily bread. My heart cries out

Joy

*Let us fix our eyes on Jesus, the author and perfecter of
our faith, who for the joy set before him endured the
cross, scorning its shame, and sat down at the right hand
of the throne of God.*
—Hebrews 12:2, NIV

And so the yearning strong,
with which the soul will long,
shall far outpass the power of human telling;
for none can guess its grace
till Love creates a place
wherein the Holy Spirit makes a dwelling.
—Bianco da Siena

Joy